This Side of Light

This Side of Light

Selected Poems (1995–2020)

Carolyn Marie Souaid

With a foreword by
Arleen Paré

Signature
EDITIONS

Cover design by Doowah Design.
Cover art by Carolyn Marie Souaid.
Photo of Carolyn Marie Souaid by Joel Silverstein.

This book was printed on Ancient Forest Friendly paper.
Printed and bound in Canada by Hignell Book Printing Inc.

We acknowledge the support of The Canada Council for the Arts and the Manitoba Arts Council for our publishing program.

Library and Archives Canada Cataloguing in Publication

Title: This side of light : selected poems (1995-2020) / Carolyn Marie Souaid ; with a foreword by Arleen Paré.
Other titles: Poems. Selections
Names: Souaid, Carolyn Marie, 1959- author. | Paré, Arleen, 1946- writer of foreword.
Identifiers: Canadiana 20220429499 | ISBN 9781773241173 (softcover)
Subjects: LCGFT: Poetry.
Classification: LCC PS8587.O87 A6 2022 | DDC C811/.54 — dc23

Signature Editions
P.O. Box 206, RPO Corydon, Winnipeg, Manitoba, R3M 3S7
www.signature-editions.com

CONTENTS

Foreword 9

SWIMMING INTO THE LIGHT (1995)

Infertility..18
Mister Falafel...19
The Palmist..20
Foreshadowing..21
Khamseen...22
The Fertile Crescent 23
Man in a Doorway II..24
Crèche Saint-Vincent-de-Paul, 2 25
La Place des Martyrs 26
rue Hamra 27
Root...28

OCTOBER (1999)

Last Thoughts of Pierre Laporte, Stuffed and Left in a
Car Trunk at St-Hubert Airbase...............................31
After the First Death..32
Mortality..33
Thursday Night...34
Escape...36
Roadrunner and Coyote..37

SNOW FORMATIONS (2002)

Sedna, Revised 41
Two Reincarnations...42
Arctic Flight 43
Baggage 44
Cabin Fever, 1..45
Dinner at Annie's 46
Stranded...48
Postcard Home, Delirium...50
Cabin Fever, 2..51
Snow Formations...52
Journal Entry..53
Stone Carver...54
The Wind, Not Nothing..55
The Airstrip 56
Throat Song..57
Canvas 58
Still, Life..59

SATIE'S SAD PIANO (2005)

Prologue...63
Mont Royal, 8..64
Venus, 3...65
Rose 66
Mont Royal, 7..69
Mont Royal...70
Letters, 3 72

PAPER ORANGES (2008)

Throat Song (Refrain)..75

Improviso...76

Rain Rain...77

Stuck in Traffic, Listening to a Yuletide Message
of the Emergency Broadcast System................................78

What Could Happen 79

Paper Oranges...80

Forty Thousand Wishes on Your Birthday.......................81

Figure Ascending 82

FGHT DPOR CY 83

My Tahiti..84

Point of No Return 85

Asleep / Awake 86

More Than a Hair..87

Afterword 88

After the Crematorium 89

THIS WORLD WE INVENTED (2015)

I

Scale.. 102

Space 103

Light 104

Context 105

Collage.. 106

II

The Holocaust Tower.. 110

School 112

The Hottest Car I Ever Drove Was a 1978 Monza
With a V8 Engine and a Fuchsia Interior 113

5 a.m. the Day of Your Mother's Funeral 114

Night Drive 115

Barkwoodby.. 116

Note... 117

Introduction to Reiki.. 118

Watching You Do T'ai Chi at Dawn 119

THE ELEVENTH HOUR (2020)

Augury, I 123

And So, the Wind.. 124

This Finite Moment 125

Autobiography 126

Augury, II.. 127

City Fountain, Remembrance Day 128

Timeline.. 129

The Black Box, Unpacked 131

Status Update.. 132

Speaking of Death 133

Arthur 134

Augury, V.. 135

Acknowledgments... 136

About the Author 137

FOREWORD

Arleen Paré

On the morning of December 25th, 1965, Carolyn Marie Souaid received a gift that would guide her life's direction. It was a small, red, leather-bound diary with a tiny gold key. And although many girls — yes, it was almost always girls — received this popular mid-century gift, not all of them made such good use of it. For Carolyn, it was lifesaving and life-altering. At the age of six she began her enduring relationship with writing: she had started to write her life. From this early age, she took writing seriously: *By the age of 12,* she says, *I was writing scripts and directing plays that my friends and I would perform on house driveways, and in backyards and barns during our summer holidays.* Concurrently she wrote poetry. In secret.

By her own admission, the poetry of her youth was *pretty bad,* but it served *as an outlet for [her] angst about being the unpopular fat kid at school.* By 15, however, she was so displeased, she piled her notebooks on the sidewalk and lit a match to them, promising herself, as Virginia Woolf had advised, *to write again only when I had real experience to write about.*

As she matured, she garnered many *real* experiences: places, positions, people, and points of view that informed her writing. The quality of her writing matured as well, exceeding simple maturity, and moving into brilliance. The interests and themes of her published poetry remained largely personal and, in the same vein as her youthful writing, she continued to write her life, publicly and seriously. Quoting Mordecai Richler, and as her subsequent collections testify, she has *always been interested in being a "faithful witness to my time and place."*

While completing her BA in English Literature at McGill from 1978 to 1981, she maintained her earnest longing to become a writer, filling journals, as she did in her youth, with poems, stories, and ideas for novels. They fell short once again, she confesses, as much youthful writing does, but they kept her dream alive.

Eventually she found herself in law school, but without much investment or interest, she soon dropped out. In her late twenties, her initial poetry publication came quickly and unexpectedly. An early poem, "no one, not even my mother, came to the wedding," appeared in *Quarry Magazine* in 1989 and that single poem, published in a quality literary journal, provided the confidence she needed to apply for a Master's in Creative Writing at Concordia University in Montreal. This allowed her to focus more earnestly on writing from 1991 to 1996 — although in the beginning, she admits, she didn't care about finishing the degree, and wanted primarily to meet other English-language writers in Montreal. So much of the literary action in Montreal at that time was happening in the French literary community. Living on the south shore in St-Lambert, a suburb of the metropolis, contributed to her feeling out of the cultural and literary loop.

Her contemporaries at the time were many of Montreal's Anglo literary luminaries: Stephanie Bolster, Gillian Sze, Susan Gillis, Carmine Starnino, Sina Queyras. However, unlike her current partner Endre Farkas's literary collective, she never felt a part of any collectivity herself.

Her writerly influences changed over time, but all have had an impact on her writing. She lists F. Scott Fitzgerald (*for his eloquent lyricism; and his depth and brevity in a single sentence*) and Samuel Beckett (*for his dark, absurd take on the human condition*). These are the writers she most admired when she was at McGill in her undergrad program.

As she began to develop her own voice, she added William Carlos Williams, whom she credits *for his democracy, his radical use of enjambment and the strong visual element in his writing.* And in her twenties, most influentially, she had discovered Charles Bukowski.

Later she included Sharon Olds, *for her ability to spin everyday language into graphic, often unsettling, portraits of family life.* She also notes Louise Glück, *for her insights into family relationships, loneliness, divorce, and death, and for her spare writing, intense discipline, and unflinching portrayal of existential despair.* Souaid adds, *I suppose I was thick into the homelife and mothering thing* (during her thirties and forties), *so perhaps that's why I gravitated to them at that time.*

As Souaid's work progressed, other writers became significant influences. Dionne Brand *for her images and beautiful use of language;* George Elliott Clarke *for his musicality, his colourful, muscled language, his social/historical consciousness, his collections woven of multiple voices;* and Billy Collins, *for making the ordinary extraordinary and for the fluidity of his writing. My latest collection,* The Eleventh Hour, *aimed for his fluidity.*

The first graduate class she took in the Concordia writing program, with Gary Geddes, covered the elements of the long poem. The long poem form resonated for Souaid, resembling, and allowing, as it does, the narrative form. This is the form she employed with great success in her first four collections, drawing readers into the diverse elements of her maturing voice and expanding life.

It was during Souaid's time at Concordia that she started writing about her life as a childless woman. This life, threaded through with her Lebanese ancestral heritage and latterly with the additional attachment through the adoption of her son who was born in Beirut, began to expand into the more generally political. She became more aware of the broad political context within which she lived. Out of her creative thesis, which won best thesis of the year at Concordia, she was able to publish her first collection, *Swimming into the Light.* This initial collection became a major poetic success for Souaid, both personally and publicly, and she became completely committed to the practice of poetry.

All her early collections were grounded in what she had studied in Geddes's long poem class. She wrote three books following *Swimming into the Light,* using what she terms "the concept album" format to construct them; each includes characters and a loose narrative arc. These first collections, *Swimming into the Light, October, Snow Formations,* and *Satie's Sad Piano* became what she considers her "early novels."

Souaid's poetry is heart-stoppingly intimate and revealing. From the publication of her first collection, she has allowed readers access into the most personal parts of her life, close to the bone, where she holds them. It would seem that her literary encounter with Charles Bukowski in her twenties gave her the licence she needed to write poems that are not only personal, but are also, appropriately, unabashedly lusty and raw. In "no one, not even my mother, came to the wedding," for instance, she writes "that raw winter, / I lured him, / spread-legged, drunk, dizzy / like a fifty-dollar whore."

As Georgia O'Keeffe once wrote, "an artist is the last person in the world who can afford to be affected," and Souaid is the one of the least affected poets I have read. Her sensuality is pure unbridled Souaid, it is simply life as she sees it, life as she lives it. She writes with teeth, always, as her brother once advised her to do — about her father. As she does in her last collection, "to write him into a book, / poetry or prose, something with teeth / that the critics will value centuries from now."

This casual, sensual intimacy, this defiance of mainstream twentieth-century mores, is one of Souaid's literary strengths, a striking component of her writerly expression. Given that few women, heterosexual or otherwise, and Susan Olds notwithstanding, have been sufficiently comfortable, sufficiently bold, to employ it, it might be seen as one of her significant poetic achievements.

Fearlessness is a hallmark of her work. Without arrogance, she writes what's meaningful to her in the moment. Without apology, she writes in her own intrepid, fierce style. Without defence, she writes as a Québécoise about the importance of Canada.

As if being Anglo-Québécoise in the late twentieth century wasn't political enough, considering what Hugh MacLennan once called "the two solitudes," given the FLQ and the PQ, Souaid's oeuvre also includes life in northern Quebec, the Inuit culture, and aspects of colonial culture there. Having spent several non-consecutive years in the North, teaching — and learning — she wrote *Snow Formations*, her third collection, about her emotional, cultural, physical, and sexual experiences in the North.

Concurrently, she lives the daily experience of an Arab / Jewish relationship with her Jewish partner, Endre Farkas. Together they produced *Blood is Blood,* a controversial videopoem dealing with the ongoing conflict in the Middle East. Her Lebanese heritage, which she shares with her adopted son, is another basic area of personal and writerly difference, raising issues of contrast and bridging between individuals and cultures. Clearly, as compelling as her personal, intimate poetry can be, Souaid's poetry is also singularly questing and baldly political.

Although early on she defined herself as a "solitary writer," without a strong cohort of local fellow writers, one of her primary concerns remained connection. Most of her early books *focused on the difficult bridging of worlds (adoptive mother/adopted child; Arab/ Jew; English/French; native/non-native). In some ways, the world I was writing about was the world of solitude (how people from opposing realities struggle to inhabit the same space despite the vast chasm that separates them). The impossibility of truly connecting with the "Other."*

Her family background and her local positionalities have placed Souaid in situations that have often intersected with a variety of momentous political events and geographies. Despite growing up in quiet communities close to Montreal, political events have been an important part of her Québécois life. Her second collection, *October,* deals with the well-known October Crisis. As a child, Souaid was a loyal Canadian whose anxieties were stirred when the Québécois revolution turned deadly. In 1970, the deputy premier of the province of Quebec, Pierre Laporte, was kidnapped and assassinated by the FLQ, a Quebec nationalist group. Laporte was kidnapped from the community where Souaid lived as a child — a mere three kilometres from her house. This brought the Quebec struggle for sovereignty very close to home for her. She uses reflection and the thorny language and religious split in Quebec as this collection's primary focus. In this collection, she includes a poem that she wrote in French, one of her early languages, in a heartfelt gesture of bridging.

Her loyalty to the then popular vision of a bilingual Canada, and especially to the iconic Pierre Elliott Trudeau, a family favourite, is clear in her fourth collection, *Satie's Sad Piano*. In it, she defends the meaning of Trudeau in Canada's history and imagination. As in so much of Souaid's writing, *(t)he language leaps off the page in exciting, vivacious rhythm and rhyme*, as ARC reviewer Yvonne Blomer relates.

Souaid began writing it immediately following his death in 2000. Using elements from Trudeaumania and the trope of several voices, she includes a forbidden love story — and an abortion. She created characters and modelled the collection after Michael Ondaatje's *The Collected Works of Billy the Kid* and George Elliott Clarke's *Whylah Falls*, both of which she was reading at the time. Not all the voices are human. She notes that she considers *Satie's Sad Piano* to be her most ambitious project to date. But she thinks, although some would disagree, that *it was also a failure in that some of the poems are incomprehensible or too obscure.*

At the same time, as occurs with fine poets, Souaid had the great good fortune to fall intensely in love with language itself. This deep regard and attachment to language is evident in all that she writes; her diction is exact, clear, specific, and lively. In each poem she chooses the best word for the thought or image, and places each word in the best order for the poem. For example, these lines from "Figure Ascending" in *Paper Oranges*, one of her later collections:

> I have no idea whose life this is
> or why the soft spot for a few thick clouds
> and nameless blooms
> that stirred me awake last spring
> through a ripped-up screen

She speaks French but writes almost exclusively in English. As a child she had friends who spoke little English. Again, bridging the two language communities was an early concern. Both her parents speak some Arabic, and since the adoption of her son, Alex, she has developed stronger ties to Lebanon.

This World We Invented, Souaid's penultimate collection, is both an act of imagination and responsibility. Like *Paper Oranges* before it, and *The Eleventh Hour*, her latest, *This World We Invented* is not themed and developed more incidentally from the poems themselves. The poems, as voiced in a 2015 *All Lit Up* interview, "zoom in and out, shifting focus to accommodate varied dimensions of experience . . . from the breakdown of a relationship to primordial ooze to a suicide bomb to a son doing his math homework. In a disarmingly personable voice, Souaid investigates our darker moments . . . often with wry humour. If our world is an imperfect invention, it is also, for Souaid, a source of wonder — where 'the trick was not to fall asleep but to notice everything / in its brevity.'"

This too: Souaid writes with angst firmly in her mind and she ensures that she shadows it on the page. Beneath almost every collection, every poem, every line, there lurks an existential worry, much like Louise Glück's "unflinching existential despair." This is not unusual; poets and poetry can be that way. Souaid is rightly aware of the "higher" questions and issues that pepper a life with existential angst. In this regard she is well-aligned with these contemporary anxious times. She is a thoroughly modern poet with a fearless, fearful vision, with the right words, right images, right metaphors, to convey her particular place in life, her particular poetic vision. As she moves out to embrace the world, those parts of the world that touch her, she draws that world for the rest of us. This is her writing her life and the overlap: this is us reading it.

SWIMMING INTO THE LIGHT
(1995)

The 'childless woman' and the 'mother' are a false polarity.
— Adrienne Rich

Our genes, ever sentimental, abhor singularity.
— Susan Glickman

Infertility

There are shapes my body will never make —
the perfect O, for instance, that women form
to expel the gleaming apricot head of a newborn

part of their own flesh & their lover's
part of their mother & father & generations
before them, swimming into the light

the whole universe from beginning to end
falling through them
like the sweet green rain.

Mister Falafel

I smoke by the January window
reflection & I

dark rinse of traffic
outside

leaning umbra
of a coffee mug

grey mushroom
wall

ashtray, a crumpled foil heart
on the table.

I smoke the cigarette, filling a small chair
with myself.

The Palmist

— for Rhonda

The moon chases the dark
for its other half.

My hands in clammy leather, the black highway
splash of cars as I wait for a bus, wait for her

to trace the fault lines
in my palm

blue TV light in a corner
of the room, soft noise

of her touch realigning the planets
birthing a child.

A fine dream of snow passes the window
& we are laughing now

huddled by the stove, fingers warming
thin china cups.

Waiting for the bus home, the top-heavy sky
lifts away. Even the crazy metal of cars
holds new meaning.

Foreshadowing

When I finally let go
of science, I remembered the story of Moses
how his own mother defied the Pharaoh
& wove her baby into a nest of bulrushes

how she let him go
as one lets go of consciousness in sleep
she, alone at the riverbed, a pinpoint
against the darkening sky
cool dry breeze emptying
the heat from her body

& I thought of the Pharaoh's daughter who found him
curled on his side like a small animal
limbs tucked under his body
twitching lightly

nameless, motherless
drifting into the wide-open
hands of God.

Khamseen*

The plane lands
like a small typhoon.

Passengers jostle on the tarmac
throats dry as cumin.

We board the mushroom darkness of a bus
raw wind bending around us

where nothing moves
but the odd molecule & Assaad's face
lifting from a dry scrap of paper.

The Syrian President
eyes us from every parched wall
of Customs. He is in every russet uniform
every cocked rifle, every broom-thick moustache

every red coal of every cigarette.

His earth-cracked lips heave & harden
under the volcano of words.

Somewhere in the desert
the small spine of a cactus
shivers.

---

*An extremely dry, stifling, sand-laden wind which originates in the North African Sahara, and lasts for approximately 50 days.

The Fertile Crescent

Bedouin women
in a cobbler's doorway
cross-legged with their baskets
of eggs & vine leaves

eyewhites, a dull glaze

babies in their laps
like steaming loaves of bread.

Death is a distant country to them
a great, green curve of land
where ancestors wait
unburdened —

mosaic of upturned faces
like golden plates of fruit
in the sun.

Man in a Doorway II

Old tawny fingers scattering the worry
along his rosary, beads blunt & smooth as bullets

who never cried when they shelled his house
not even when he lifted his son's head
by its twisted nape & carried him out of the fire.

He rests under the tired hood
of his eye. This is God's will
it seems to say.

I pity him. Shorn white head, the way his reverent
toes curl under the frayed hemp of his sandals.

Around him the street is levelled. Chances are
he won't live to see the new world rise up
from the rubble, brassy cafés
with bold awnings & gilt-edged tables
where men in fine suits will smoke & haggle
over cobalt-blue thimbles of Arabic coffee
afternoon clouds rearranging the sky.

I memorize the scene
like some mantra.

This making & unmaking of the world.

Crèche Saint-Vincent-de-Paul, 2

For a moment, there is nothing
in the air but a dumb gaze
like that instant after a relative dies
as one kneels in the half-light
by the ashen corpse, breathless

then a faint stir as the soul lifts
& crosses out of the darkness.

I wait on the cool green marble
sun angling down from a tall window
moment filled with coughs & echoes of coughs
& the long bar of light streaming in & then
a nun in her blue habit
materializes at the door.

In that first breath we take together
I have already memorized
every detail of you, every nuance, the fine weave
of your hair, each nutmeg-brown stitch
the pale pink braid of your skin.

Deep inside my body
the first pulse of you.

La Place des Martyrs
(1991)

They gather here
as though a party were about to break, anarchy
of card tables & broken lawn chairs
soda pop & cigarettes.

Or perhaps the party is over & the rubble
is really the aftermath of a good time, champagne toss
of peanut shells & confetti on New Year's Eve.

A man licks an ice-cream cone
another shuffles randomly, wondering what to sweep
leftover kids straddle the chipped wings of a statue.

16 years of war
200,000 dead.

Everyone moves cautiously in his skin
waiting for the hangover to set in.

rue Hamra

Slit-eyed in shadeless West Beirut
combing maps for a sign
a landmark, any point of reference
the day, a haze
of dust & coriander.

The driver circles & circles for parking
wiping oil from his forehead, drops
us somewhere to pick through
olive-grey boards & fallen plaster
baby gathered into my breasts, into the very nucleus
of my being, the pressure of his weight
entering me, every rosy particle of matter
the sunny planet of his face.

Soon the world begins
to fall away from us, spinning on its own congested axis
as though we no longer need it
the noise, the traffic, the silvery-white light
as though we can finally be everything
to each other

the sun, the moon, the stars.

Root

How I saved your umbilical cord
in a Birks box, wrapped in tissue
with your first shoes & a lock of hair

how when my mother bathed you it fell away
& she delivered it on a bed of Kleenex
part of the tree from which you hung like amber fruit
in another woman's womb

how my mother's shining eyes met mine

how she handed it to me the way a neighbour
shares a clipping from her garden
hoping it will take root.

OCTOBER
(1999)

Two old races and religions meet here and live their separate legends, side by side. If this sprawling half-continent has a heart, here it is.
— Hugh MacLennan, Two Solitudes

Last Thoughts of Pierre Laporte, Stuffed and Left in a Car Trunk at St-Hubert Airbase

Their jackal eyes, their cool
upturned collars

the holy chain on my neck, my wife, my kids
my lamplit bungalow

downtown drunks and their pointless lives
like beads of a broken rosary
pinging across the floor

Domtar men with heart conditions, midnight jobs
stirring soupy vats of paper

forebears on the stony land
ragged, broken men

livestock bred into madness

the world tipped on its side
unstoppable, the whirring
in my brain

the suffocating darkness

just wanting a pillow
and a last grab of air.

After the First Death

When someone dies, all you can do
is lie in bed
like a worm of toothpaste, wincing
at the clinical starch of day —

grating sunlight on the walls, metallic
voices on the radio.

He's in the dark drawer, eyes frosted shut.
Body like a cold potato in the ground.

You know it will always be this way.

One man dead. Another — your uncle —
on his way out. Eyewhites yellowing
in the hospital bed.

All of a sudden, your mother's meatloaf
will stop tasting right
and Sundays will leave you
saddened at the wilting vine
on an autumn fence or the absent sun
like a dead piano key.

Dead, no matter how hard you bang it.

Mortality

Every sound, every small vibration
is a lesson from God, a reminder
of our own slim time
on earth

utterings of the sudden beginnings
and endings of things —

radio voices rising and falling
over the airwaves

a hairbrush
slipping from my mother's grasp

the firecracker static
of socks on a dry rug

her quivering hand
on the doorknob

the words *We have to tell the children*

my heart starting up
like a thousand soldiers
drumming off to war

our neighbour's mean yellow dog
roughing up a garbage can

Dad's restless weight
on the bedspring

the house quietly draining
of light.

Thursday Night

Days after the murder: we were driving
home from Brownies, stars all jumbled up in the sky
when it happened — Mister Shaughnessy went ballistic on me
for speaking French to Nathalie who didn't know
a word of English.

Everybody speaks White in this car! he snapped
and all of us just sat there, trembling
in the divided air,

small of our backs
stapled against the cold vinyl.

My mind reeled: What brother turned on a brother?
How depraved did you have to be
to actually kill someone
with your bare hands?

For a split second, there was a frightening imbalance
in the air, then he simply lost control
of the wheel. I felt the blood drain
from me as we roared up the sidewalk
and then I heard the body of the car crumple
like a piece of cardboard.

He jammed on the brakes.

I thought of lunging at him, my pronged ring
leaving viperous dots of blood on his cheek,
I thought of a cold knife pressed against the base
of his throat, I thought of its starry blade
making a quick fish-slit, I thought unflinchingly
of everything.

I waited a moment, and then the huge animal
inside me
fell silent.

Escape

In the recurring dream, I am locked
in my cupboard under the sink,
hot-water pipes leaving twin burns
along my wrists.

I am headed
nowhere

like the snaking line
of the damned

inching
decimal by decimal
into oblivion

or the murdered man
bumping around in a car trunk,
feet blundering
north, south, east, west
like the fibrillating compass
of his head.

In the dream, my hands are tied
while the killers go free

memorizing a trap door
in the horizon

popping the padlock and reappearing,
unmanacled, to the bright nod of camera lights,
to flares along the runway
and their brilliant getaway
planes.

Roadrunner and Coyote

Two empty wineglasses, the cat in his quiet corner
lapping up yesterday's meal —   this is the cockeyed world
as you entered it

early this morning
when you crept downstairs with a blanket
and your ragamuffin toy.

Your dad gunning out of the driveway.
Me, by the kitchen sink, waiting for daylight
to come crawling back.

This is the scene you passed up

for television and a few laughs, the ongoing spat
between Roadrunner and Coyote.

At your age, you've already decided that none of it is real —
the cartoon sky, the insubstantial poof Coyote makes
when he hits the ground

the boulder tailing him relentlessly off the cliff
gathering momentum, like a dark
freefalling storm cloud.

Somehow, you know that nothing
 — especially not the flimsy cocktail parasol
he's holding over his head —

will save him.

SNOW FORMATIONS
(2002)

The greatest poverty is not to live in the physical world.
— Wallace Stevens

Sedna, Revised

One by one, you swallowed
the rotted-out boats,
gobbled them whole
like babies.

Underwater, your eyes decayed,
your brain turned black. Your hair
tangled with the plants
and snaked
across emptiness.

Cold-blooded mermaid,
what if this were your story:

What if nature had delayed
your curved hips, the inevitable
fleshing-out of sex?

Picture *terra firma*, your new life:
thighs crayoned pink, the dormant pearl
still snugly in place.

Running, you flee the wolves in your skirt,
the blushing hillside,

the sun, whose scandalous light
will leave you cold.

Two Reincarnations

1.

Winter paws the room white.
Your shy self, once-removed,
strays in.
Sheepishly.

Whose January are you?

Whose unshackled sky?

2.

Don't underestimate the subtlety
of snow. Winter shocks the clenched mind,
dislocating neurons.

Note how the merest hole in a cloud
becomes a gateway, a door.

How one simple flake
triggers an entire blizzard.

All those years of unremembered light
avalanching through a crack.

And just yesterday
I had the world figured out.

Arctic Flight

January limped in like an old crone:
haggard snow, a weak pulse
of sky through the skinny trees.

All last fall, the graveyard leached
into the water table. Leaves wallowed
in their own waste. Soon,
even the birds were spent.

I myself flew
into exile —

way north of the trees
with a knapsack, and a bottle of brandy
in my eiderdown coat

stared from the small plane
as my fissured, brown
liver-spotted town
vaporized in the dark air

and when I woke, the world had accumulated again
outside my window

the strapping, white, freshness of it
shovelling life
back into my eyes.

Baggage

The world is slower and duller than I thought.
And those travelling pockets of excitement in the sky,
ribbons and party bags, are nothing

but clouds. Did you know the Inuit have no words
for 'forecast' and 'certainty'?
I might have dreamt that.

I've had plenty of time to sleep.

What I know: each day
stiffens another crust of bread.
Count on nothing.

Count back to zero.

five, four, three

Think: warm water, chamomile.

two

Think: slow
Himalayan climb.

one, zero —
serenity.

I wait for my things to arrive, rationing
patience, raisins,

country
(yawn)
& western.

Cabin Fever, 1

It was me, myself, in the mirror.
It was the empty wineglass on the table.
And the curtained window, like a drawstring
on the world. It was the dogless
horizon, the recurring spaces between clouds.
It was the gale force ripping through
colour, salmon and cerulean flattened
into monotones. It was the grey void of water,
the one wrong step to certain death. It was the frozen
membrane starting up again, the coming dread —
next week, next month, the cold shoulder
of snow against the door, the house,
the entire hamlet. It was what I was waiting for,
what would never come, something, anything
to neutralize the chill. It was thoughts of my mother
in a spring dress, days behind in her correspondence.
All her drawers of empty blue envelopes.
It was footprints, receding; their zeroes
growing fainter and fainter.

It was me, myself, in the mirror.

Dinner at Annie's

I mouth them with a pure heart,
smackingly — *muskox, caribou.*
Others, too.
Lemming.

Do you know how much life slips away
uncatalogued each day? How many words.
Warm clot of mother's milk.
       I didn't mean words, I meant heft.
The sinewed world.

How did my convoluted journey
get me here? Guest in a strange home.

       A tool on page nine of *Getting to Know
the North* arrives in my hand. Moonshaped,
for cutting.

Observant, they would have caught me
gloating. Schooled in such trivia.

Need I remind you how the brain responds?

Involuntarily, and with passion.
Conspiring, as always, with the tongue.
Having learned an expression
or two. Simple nouns.
Ulu.

Did no one hear me?

Tuktumik takuvunga.

An eye turns. Another turns
into the light, checking a toenail. Concurrently,

dinner opens up on the floor, rations on the tough hide
of a box slit along the seams. The rest is all basic
vocabulary: kneel, gnaw, scrape, slurp.
Bodily stuff. Punctuated by silence.
Fart. Burp.

Long story short: a good table. Animal parts
shorn and tossed, a slurry
of bones and fat.

Deep in the small of my back,
vibrations from the next room.
Someone's brambly throat
headed for a clearing.

As though a voice were on the way.

Stranded

Someone miscalculated the day.
      Or purposely put us to the Test.

Gave us one measly boat to defend ourselves
against those conniving rocks, slicing through the rapids
like fins. We saved ourselves, and camp floated in
on a risky patch of land

just as the miserable clouds
netted the last of our light.

Days we were stuck there with nothing to do
but count the accidents
of nature,

the number of blueberry stains on our hands, and how many times
a day we rinsed out the same tin cup. We counted
our steps to the pee-hole, our steps
from here to there — to drinking water so cold
it seared our hands.

Mostly, we shivered in the damp tent
as the weather collapsed around us.

That's when we began to hallucinate — saw God's mean face
in a thundercloud, literally caught His fickle hand
pouring a flask of rain all over us.
We watched our guides empty the rum,
watched the storm bulge up
inside them, their savage bodies crossing the line
into roaring madness, floundering hell,

on and on and on
until finally misplacing themselves
in a big senseless heap on the floor.

At dawn, we awoke to the volatile sun.

Postcard Home, Delirium

Anyone sane would ask the question.
What's a choppy 8-millimetre film doing outside
my window? And who are those windblown actors
flying across my screen, sped-up, grainy,
clutching one another for dear life?

The phones are dead, so I'm writing you this
huddled against a lantern with my flask
of Southern Comfort. Listen.
Can you hear it?

Flapping celluloid. The crinkled
minus-60 air.

Trust me. This is no bit part, it's the role of a lifetime:
mummy in a sleeping bag,
staving off the chill.

Never mind.

I could have been an ice cube
or a solitary flake. Blue-breath frost
on the earth's white brain.

Haven't seen the sun in months.
Wish you (it) were here.

Cabin Fever, 2

Outside, flustered snow
caught in a crisscrossing wind.

Every night, the same tune. Stereo playing
its slow saxophone
for my drowsing mug of gin.

Lamplight's languid glow
on the walls.

My orange cat in a half-moon
licking itself to sleep. Or —

snapshot of

my orange cat in a half-moon
licking itself to sleep.

The record is

skipping. None of us is
going anywhere.

Down south,
        it's spring.

Snow Formations

Pale light drifts
over puffs of snow

tugging at the eye,
the sleepy heart.

Your hand travels
into mine,

tracing every line
and curve.

Even in death there is life,
you say.

Listen to the way   *silence*

fills up with   *silence*

;

listen to the dunes

:

they are talking to you.

Journal Entry

Naming it "the best day of my life"
I was recalling the trapped wind in my boots,
my ballooning hood. The prudish moon
spying down on us from the sky.

I wanted to record the drama in my heart, my head,
winged burst of light, the *whorling*. I wanted

you, no —

I wanted language, Orwellian precision.
The words *spiral, concentric, ringed*
pelvic heat.

I wrote and wrote, grabbed challenge

by the throat, wanting it all
on paper, frozen,

a moment in time, exactly:

fresh dung on the snow, curled heap
of earth and steam;

my lips and tongue rounding your fingers,
oil, blood,

the snared fox in my mouth,
dithering.

Stone Carver

There is much that happens (between) the time the stone is found
and the time the people in the south see it as a bird or anything.
— Paulosie Kasadluak

Not you, but one of you,
is dead. Hours ago,
while the sky was still

green as stone,

a half-dozen fault lines
running through it.

One village north, a chirping
bullet found his head.
Apparently, all she had said,
his white lover, was: *no.*

Striking a raw nerve. Chipping
away at him. He left no note,

no apology. Nothing
(for the Guild of Crafts)

but two sculptures. One on the bureau,
free-form creature
towering into flight;

the second, lifeless on a pillow,

the manna lifted
right out of it.

The Wind, Not Nothing

It's not in the steady pull of light toward you, but in
the first instant, the flash, when suddenly you recognize
the capacity for ugliness and beauty
under one roof. Whitefish. Rusty cigarette foil
floating backwards in the sea. What it all means
for the silvered brain. To harbour interconnectedness:
a man dies and the rest of the world goes on thrashing
someplace else. To see deception in all its prisms: snowflakes
and their glass houses. A loved one, cutting you.
To stare into someone's downcast eyes and still see
summer's compassionate hours: the delicate
browns of flowering mushrooms. Scruff returning
to the fold. Arctic heather. A gull, say, and his wan shadow,
traipsing after the wind.
The wind, I said — not
nothing.

The Airstrip

I stare through a small window,
registering your face one last time, your composure
in the violent start-up of the engine,
long black hair flying.

What we both desired — my body
filled with child

— was impossible.
Simplicity.

Tomorrow, the moneyed world will come jangling back
and the bloodsucking banks,
like my relatives,
will all be smiling my way.

Even the ordinary sun
will be issuing orders: eat, sleep, work.

It is blustering madness as we lift away.

Moments later, from the sky,
the turbulent snow is serene again,
tranquil.

You seem to be waving, hushed
blue shadow of the plane
passing over you.

How could I refuse your kiss, the one
gift without any strings attached?

Throat Song

It was the end of God and abstractions, my last year
in school. Dusk penetrating a shingled
beach house. The suffocating
humidity.

Bedside, a few thin volumes. Beckett and
his dark oeuvre.

      Who knows how it happened, or why —
a mysterious bird arrived on my sill
like so much light,

puffing up his chest,

the raspberry sky
speaking mountains
through him.

Shifting my attention to the salted particulars:
algae, starfish,
the ordinary
granular sea
out there.

Making the wait /
weight bearable.

Canvas

In the end, only the beach can speak
for itself. All day, I watched the sun
scald and bleach.

The sky whipped up a storm
of gulls. Shapeless, unassuming,

white is the tufted breath of clouds,
silence feathering in
where words leave off.

White is effortlessly white.

At dusk, the sea left
its foamy configuration
in the sand.

All day I waited,
but my thoughts wouldn't turn into poems.

Still, Life

From the graveyard everything looks good.
Shrouded, now, in white,
crystallized, I see that.
I also see carbonized snow
as a good thing.

Pardon my cynicism, my failure to acknowledge this
sooner. I'll get to the point.

How many of us ever take time to enjoy
the Earth's exquisite intricacies? Victorian lace.
Spiderwebs. The organza wing
of a common fly.

Who, among us, actually hears bracelets
in the chilly wind? A rattlesnake
coiling through light?

Put it this way.
Next time you claim to be bored,
visualize brownish, blackish, grim nothingness
and then feed on the world,
one breath at a time. Imagine the tang
of unusual spices on your tongue;
red dust falling
lightly
from a powdered stamen.

Loosen the flower, drink some wine,
make your solemn declaration
singingly —

I can't even imagine not being here.

SATIE'S SAD PIANO
(2005)

Es tan corto el amor, y es tan largo el olvido.
— Pablo Neruda

Love is so short, and forgetting is so long.

Prologue

The New Millennium

The bishops feared a dip on Wall Street,
flash floods, tornadoes, snow squalling
in tongues, the chickens awry,

— a white, interstellar madness.

They predicted the harvest in tatters,
provisions under the staircase
stupefied into dust.

The prescient would hear it coming:
a week early, demons in the glassware,
heirloom dinner plates shifting
imperceptibly,

a chink in the rattling air.

They feared 40 days & 40 nights
of blighted non-believers
spitting up blood, bile, the Seven Deadly Sins
of the rainbow

bruised & shaken, the last conscious radio
issuing prayers for the End.

But midnight came & went, dragging its long face,

& spring arrived, as always: seeded
with light.

Mont Royal, 8

In his basement flat, a man puts the final touches
to a letter. Editing words, two or three at a time,
until his erratic pulse flattens
into greytone across the page.

The trick is to avoid emotion, erase doubt

especially now, at this critical juncture.
When strolling couples flock the censored light,
drawing momentum

from the vigorous spurt of fall —
scarlet ruckus of leaves, fighting
to hang on. Taking their cue

from even the slightest things: field mice.
Their excitable whispers scuttling the wind.

Upstairs, a rose is dying.

Or trying to. Still too stubborn,
too flushed with time
to let a gentle tug,
magnetic earth, pull it under.

Venus, 3

everything points to your
absence:

dimmed tail lights of cars & outgoing geese
the grim, subtracted leaves

a bristled, Andean chill to the air

you on exotic soil
                    — I, exiled

in the long, wan shade
of home

metaphors not of sadness, really

but of the enormity
of unneeding you

this late in the afternoon

Rose

1

Did the shroud of dawn
awaken you?

Or was it the cunning
wind of Hades, come to you

in sleep, whispering dreams
of earth

trodden & worn to ash?

A word
alone
can veil all hope

&

death is just another day
we open to.

2

Don't be surprised. I'm still here,
webbing the dark with every other abomination:
the two-headed, the rancid,
the upside-down. Fuzzy approximations
spidering God's spare rooms.

What we lack in heft, we provide in wit.

I'm the aborted air, atomized.
The sea's frail spume.

I'm the insufficient light at your back.
Here, not in breath, but in the speechless murk
in the marsh of your tongue. Dwarfed, fallow

because I couldn't assimilate, couldn't swallow
the stretch marks on the planet.
The compromised sun.
Dogs, all of you, salivating to a bell.

Your curt, manufactured smiles for the photographer.

Like them, I pictured a different hell:
The wholesome world, warmth, a bed.

Days before my birth hour, I stood outside
your apartment walls, weeping.

3

Beyond the instant, there is history,
loss, rooted in the gene pool of a city,
rusted into its ancestry.

You smell it in the air.

The elusive Northwest Passage, a scarcity
of tea. Greenish, stegosaural hulks nailed
over the river: the Navigators.
Jacques Cartier, Champlain.

Les filles who set sail, uncanonized.
Oxidizing on infant soil.

This is what lushes life,
fleshes it out.

Each moment, part of a greater genealogy.
Branch after branch twigging backwards
to the ghost nugget.

Gentrify the industrial park, but in its heart
of hearts, a condo is still an abattoir.

Take a moment like this.
You are alone, driving recklessly.
The radio is on, and you are all ears.
There is talk:

Trudeau has died.

Your sadness, shock, shatters the singularity.

Mont Royal, 7

The other image, unshot,
is the one in her mind, digital

diorama of arctic precision.
Where, limned by the sun,

celestial, she's a ray too bright
for the human eye, white

tulle gown filling the frame
with largesse.

Her happiness multiplied
substantially.

Infectious.

As when baby's breath,
startled from the bush,

confettis

into asterisks &
exclamation marks.

Excessive thrill
of snow in the air.

Mont Royal

1

You ask with trepidation —
how time wizens to this.
Rigor mortis. Life's crushed years in a box.
A rose, face down in the dust,
shrunken, black.

Knowing his fate, Icarus
in the labyrinth, longing to fly,
you wonder —
would he have borne the showy wings,
the rush & ride of beginnings,

would he have chanced the sky?
Would he have bested Kerouac, nerving
for madness on a cock-fool whim,
the sun's mescaline kiss
at his back?

— *Yes.*

2

Yes, she said, her winged heart pumping
beyond the metronome

&

the measured, onward beat of modernity.
Loathing the riff of temperate company girls.

Yes to Marrakesh & mangoes, she said.

Yes to the madrigal sky & to life
            pointing like a gun at her head,

opening fire, fortissimo.

Letters, 3

By what right do I commune with the hooded monks,
my modest chapel stained in blood?

What divine light do I gather here
in full menstrual éclat?

Sweetened in my underthings. Undeserving.

Hours snake through the chaste dome
while I shed my skin, shameless in my slither down

from God to Man.

To the amphibian Sacrament. Where monster-headed

and in declension, I drink of the chalice
that pours abundance into the arched gateway

of my throat. Hymn flooding through me,
marrying the wet knot of heaven

between my thighs.

PAPER ORANGES
(2008)

Throat Song (Refrain)

Darkness. A tree. Dry grass husks.

Until.

Who knows how it happened, or why —
a goldfinch arrived like so much
light, puffing up his chest,

the raspberry sky
speaking mountains
through him.

And the miracle wasn't plankton
or the white tulle flounce of sea,
it wasn't God
clothed in the everyday breath of earth,

the miracle was the weight
itself, suddenly bearable.

Improviso

First things first: we averted life.
Then we averted death, spinning

into & out, mostly out, of control.

How else explain incoherence
but for the cumulous gods sent to flatten us
on the freeway?

We shot past the manic snow
to our February hacienda.
My feet were ice. The bed was night.

Somewhere between heaven & hell
we rode the squall, swirling

swerving. Just this side of light.

Rain Rain

Rain in the lilac. Rain
off the split white birch.
Pecking rain. Rain
in the garbage.

Forty days & forty nights.

Rain on all species, visible &
invisible. The saved & the unsaved.
Dog-shake, flyaway rain. Pearl rain.
Rain on the moon.

Mauve, missing-him rain
in her hair.

Stuck in Traffic, Listening to a Yuletide Message of the Emergency Broadcast System

Take Pi to a billion decimal places and we're still
adding to the string. Events in geologic time now occur
in the eyeblink of a human life.

We're waiting for the Answer.

Years ago, seventy thousand or so, ice sheets
moved across America, forever altering the Earth.
We're a paranoid nation on the wrong bandwidth,
fearful of Armageddon
and the suspected terrorists in our ovaries.

We obsess over pattern and causality,
read cancer into the white painted lines of the road:
zero point zero zero
zero zero — do you understand?

No matter what, southbound is a bad bet.

Tomorrow, stay put.
Throw some logs into the fire.

Dream your little dreams of the giftwrapped Hand
guiding the kingdom to its perfect end.

What Could Happen

trust the hamlet hemmed in green
trust the covered nest & august drinks
on your perfect lawn

better this
than the frayed horizon
the ambiguous trees
nothing to hang your hat on
as the distant bell
goes off in your head
some thursday
when you find yourself
picking at a stray thread
on your sleeve
the tailored light
about to unravel, taking you
to an undefined place
in the heart: a hell
for which there is no word
no cordoned-off grass

just a territorial wind
that would rip the roof
off your life
dashing the circuitry
the dog the kids
in a tangled orbit

avalanching

Paper Oranges

You're trapped in the cage,
the weather, life, against you:
sleet's ermine shawl,
groundhogs making meat
of your pumpkin. It's defeat
everywhere you look:
lean muskrat gardens, graveyards
of mangled sinks and telephones.
Not once, but twice, you mistook
your son for an iPod.

You're desperate to believe in God
but what inhabits you, locked
behind a chain-link fence
is the blinkety-blank road,
the same slovenly dog
mutating into something bigger
and uglier each day
hoarding the inadequate light.

You long to wake up just once
with an original thought
in your head, an image,
some beautiful impossibility

: paper oranges.

Forty Thousand Wishes on Your Birthday

To be universal, to be the scandalous
burn-your-bra snarl in the yard:
jungle of exploded pollen

to take the blushing, grenadine moon
in your mouth

to stroke the velvet, vulva harps
of girls, to watch men
watch you in violet desire

to map Ecuador on your belly
to rub your bullet wounds
with spiders and arsenic

to lie porous in a capricorn sarcophagus

amorous Morning at the foot of your bed,
brushing her hair.

Figure Ascending

I've no idea whose life this is
or why the soft spot for a few thick clouds
and nameless blooms
that stirred me awake last spring
through a ripped-up screen

And now   yes,   that I mention it

further signs —
footprints, handprints
in the field,
weeks of worm-fed rain
upon the squelch through which

a morning mist would someday rise.

FGHT DPOR CY

The days those days were a brown scroll
of paper towel and missives on mugs
in factory lunchrooms across the nation

never mind the soap dispensers made in China,
nothing working right anymore.

A piped-in message, largely ignored,
made a brave return, later, in a fortune-cookie:

Change your perspective, it said.
Activate Imagination's alphabet.

First, I worried about a wrong move
wreaking havoc at the Pentagon,
a Monday war

but even the masses
with their dull minds understood
there are no coincidences.

Letters on my coffee cup joined in solidarity,
issuing proclamations: Fight the Diaspora

Send in a Bright Battalion of Oranges
Puncture the Armour of Kitchens and Knives

Hang a New White Bulb over the City.

My Tahiti

I'll know when to pack up and call it a life.
Plumbing the depths of my January cocoon
I'll do it in style, in my best summer whites.
Don't expect it to be on Saturday night,
it might be midweek, say Tuesday
in a raging snowstorm. Instinct will tell me
the time has come to put it away
in the bottom drawer with my winter wools.
A bright blue package will arrive with an invitation
to comb the dumpster for my island paradise —
ferns and wild banana trees, beatnik fauna.
Coconuts growing sideways under the lucid stars.
I'll pour a flute of pomegranate wine,
watch *Casablanca* one last time,
the room adrift, the mind in
Gauguin's aquarium light.

On the runway, a plane will be waiting.

Point of No Return

You're at that point on the journey, familiarity
waning with every click of the speedometer.
You no longer know which negligible
pile of brick is actually your old house.
It could take days to find your way back,
despite the elastic light. The spaniel you left
pattering in the sprinkler
might as well be dead for all he remembers you.
It takes all your oomph just to call him,
and even then, the name catches in your throat
like a small burr, gets belligerent
with the wind, jousting a little
before getting sucked under your Michelins.
Through the rearview mirror,
you're suddenly aware of firewood
jumping off your truck, a couple
of grey canisters, your old man's tackle.
You don't even care
that you are swerving. What was once a dot
on the map is now less than an afterthought,
a box of spare parts
banging together in the dark:
your neglected porch swing, a moth angry
with its light bulb. Right now,
the instant is all you know: the sun
breaking out, contented fieldstone.
An elm in the distance, springing new growth.
The secret is not looking back.

Asleep / Awake

...unlike the ivy, I die if I attach myself.
— *André Breton*

The light has changed, though it's ill-advised to say
this is summer, this is winter.
True enough, there are burial pits
where men have gone from pink to black
in the eyeblink that history calls "eons."

Your father, like fathers past, will die.

Knowing this, acting on instinct,
the bird inside you, sad and frightened of change,
seeks solace in the natural world:
clustered hills, the solid horizon.

The good news is the Continuum, what is best understood
by allowing the universe to expand.

Seasons bleed into one another.
People pass from hospital bed into Spirit,
sometimes painfully.

In England, archaeologists excavated shards
of criminals, mostly young men,
executed four centuries ago: bits of a twelve-year-old
hanged and buried face down in a moat, another
whose skeletal fist
held the last black stump of a cross.
Also, two sawn-off crania, minus
the skulls they were once attached to.

By all accounts, the sun returned
and the lilacs, it seems, opened anyway.

More Than a Hair

for Artie Gold

Take the elastic medley of your name —
the skin stretches in spite of my short-lived brain
&   later,   much,   round & round it will go
                    the best vinyl record of the times

          I hardly knew you, but for a phone call once

from the ER, where panic flew
& for a beat, I shelved the typeset bones of your life
gathering mites in the book-filled crates
of a mouldy shop, several shops

          coherence from you, above all, above
the ceremony of x-ray machines & hissing syringes,
your brief on how to help a friend
prone to losing things trace his way from the car
back to his missing key

the abbreviated cosmos in under a minute
complete in a coffee spoon, in the shrinking light
through a coin booth:
your final beautiful chemical waltz
just days before you checked out.

Afterword

Closer to death we become Earth, sipping the dregs
in her bottom drawer: soup bowl of doddering swans,
the last sour grapes from a vine.
Seven days of zilch, seven of hypothermia.
This is how we wait, semi-alert, frost setting in while rats
grind their diamond teeth into glass. Windows once
heralded spring; now make vows they can no longer keep.
Stars extinct, art extinct,
the need to turn centuries of children (ransacking garbage)
into a fairy tale has dwindled into the spoiled night.

The world is tired.
But I, with ink and a small pad, wan and weak, would still write
a singing epilogue, a postscript in memoriam.
Friend, I might say. Note the moon straddling a tear
while the salt sea, born this late into jail and starved for water,
beckons. Treasure the quelled trees, the dry wharf split in half.
Man has fallen once or twice,
but still, with the birds, he rises at dawn.
Think. Where would we be without drive, verve,
this moored light waiting in the heart?

After the Crematorium

La beauté sera CONVULSIVE ou ne sera pas.
— *André Breton*

The morning of the crematorium
I awoke,
seasons of the palest branch
within reach
my face, in sleep,
having pushed into your autumn hair
lips first, then a cheek, an ear
these being your finest days, here
for a last leap &
we twined & moved into one another
as though it were the first time, the last
your neck smelling faintly of ovens & ash
the telephone springing with news
of the crematorium & directions
on how to get there.

Lured away, disconnected
you brushed past with your hair
or this indigo thought
of your hair in my mouth

left talking messages to yourself
notes & grocery lists
pinned to the refrigerator

as though order would beget order
laid it all out for me, later
on Post-its:

Short & sweet at the crematorium,
you'd say. One minute he was here, the next —

In fact, a painfully slow braise.

Hours wedged in the jaws of a "whale"
strand by strand, released,

the body unfurling like ribbon.

That afternoon as he cooled into winter light,
Chet Baker from the stereo
fogged up your window.

I floated in your dozing arms
above the February freeze,
my inner trumpet building
to springtime's leggy fields

to Giverny, where
          blooming, blossomed, I ran
carrying what I'd been carrying around
all these months
the huge box that is not a box
but the love that is always you
all gauze & gossamer

fluid as a jazz trail, as a bedouin song
lifting in death —

"Drift blue" or LIVE without any chance
of parole, without wings, get lost, go beyond
the warmth of down
move into each other's mythical sun,
crown it in your palm & cherish.

Then, drumbeat, the unmentionable,
gloom & doom, Chet — oh yes,
the real showstopper.

No one said, but we all knew
about the heroin in your blood
the morning that smashed across your balcony
when hope entered my left ear
a city coming straight for me
your estranged voice in all that sharded light
plunging me into the caves of my own dawn
where a piano still played
&
I couldn't help fondling that solemn place
because I had with me the seeds
of that greater package,
a few yellow notes in my hand
chirping down through the clouds.

All I ever wanted to do was become light.

Voices small & heard
            on the day of my birth:
low distant hills sending up signals,
quivering notes of brass & fire

I remember the solid road
with my walking stick & a good pair of shoes
until unexpectedly the earth gave way
the great plates shifting underfoot
& upward I shot into the sky
agitating the clouds

            clamouring, clamouring

as though the next moments
for someone else utterly depended on it
& now, well, now…

I spilled the hopelessness of "blue"
said you must feel it, too, but —
I stopped
half-expecting you to say it first:
how the sun has learned from me its rays, its intensity
the way I arch my back
for the sheer pleasure.

And whether you went down on me
then & there
or in the wicks of your eyes
you were telling me with your telling look
that you loved my glow
how I radiate happiness
how the idea of my hands
around that sacred box
strings you along
how when it finds its way
all this mantled love
into the most unnameable parts of you
it is merely a hand
needing to be where it is needed.

Secrets: I know humming rooms
louder than the average brain, I have keys
I know tedium & the slog of drifting
backwards through time

that God goes and changes the record on us is slog
that Chet got cut off before the end is slog
that still you're not home is slog, too
slog was even slog all those hours ago
at the crematorium, hours ago
in bed before anything

before the telephone woke us up
before the radio woke us up
before thoughts of becoming
bags of dust woke us up
before the generator went on
before the lights went on

when all signs of the day
pointed to more
than a dull grey walk through the snow.

9 o'clock, where are you? Why resist a lithe wine
on the tongue, the firmest purple grape?

I despise my slow demise,
the sloth of apartment clocks
reminding me reminding me reminding me
of my ticking cells that expire with the wait

nothing changes my skin needing your scent
my breath needing your eyes
I drink you especially, especially
when you're Lost.

What urge beyond magnetic pull?
What secret, interstellar code among souls?

An enigma unsolvable:

the chemistry of leaf & leaf
rubbing up against love

wet & wet

Knowing all this,
how are stillness & death viable choices?

Isn't the point that jittery uncertainty
when blade nicks skin
the very first time
when the man, larger-than-life,
dips his heart in an unfamiliar scent?

Isn't it about the purity of risk?

Once your hot sweet nest
is laced with the run-off melt
the dew from him nearing you

once you taste, once you smell
the weight of him
you'll not turn your back
on the lusty stars

you'll never say no
to the candy of earth.

What greater gift than snow on snow,
a tenor sax, the electric charge before you enter

a room, the door about to speak,
the atoms unstable,
dangerously unmaking themselves

        helixing

into a staircase of bugled light
opened to the cosmos
the balloon of Man, ascending.

Both of us there, beyond ourselves
orbiting the outermost limits of skin.

It overflows the cup, spills outward
across the continents,
flooding the immensity of earth: this want

for small trembling voices when *he touches her.*

But when finally he deserts her
      (and he will) once & for all
taking with him
the airbrushed fields
the afternoon around her heart

      what then?

She can't, won't imagine
walking hand in hand
with the turtle days of August,
the arrested trees

loses herself, for now,
in the poem:

I am the black wedding apple
I am not the fish you meant to catch
do not throw me back,
savour the worms
sprouting blithely from within.

What if you were really gone?

I pictured this as you waved goodbye
at the ovens, mask weighing down
"saying" in your own mute way

stoic on the outside, tenderly within
where a thin grass grows.

Maybe you coughed or cleared your throat
maybe you blushed, maybe
in that instant before they opened the doors
you shielded your eyes from the blaze
maybe for a split second you thought about me

more accurately

wondered what you've done to suddenly
deserve the light pouring down on you.

Graced with intelligence, living
inside the head, we codify our days.
The merest events deepen into metaphors.

A word at the bright portal, even a thought
extends beyond itself to become a sign.

I say this in all sincerity:
I'd winter with the worms, truncated.
Surrender my last dime of heat — to you.

Happily rooted.
Happily pulsing below the surface, happily giving.
Asking little in return.

Hear me day & night from even the darkest caverns.
I'm the noisy sun, my summer stretched
to bursting.

What some might call the harbinger of life:
blushing poppies. An impressive but irregular
species of bird, airborne.

Read my lips.
Today I saw my heart on a billboard.

THIS WORLD WE INVENTED
(2015)

I

Concept has form.
— *Kit White,* 101 Things to Learn in Art School

Scale

Africa was an inch and a half wide on my ruler.
The teacher smiled and pasted something into my book,
either a gold star or a moth with exceptional markings,
I don't recall.

She died. Lots of people died.
Push-pins came off the map, but more went in.
Overnight, the population doubled.
Where sprightly children once leapt about,
there were meaner ones
who excelled at games —

tagging a hapless ant with a magnifying glass,
funnelling the sun into a prick of light
as the scrabbling insect shrivelled
into seed.

It was, of course, the same destiny that awaited Joshua,
whose miraculous entry into the human race began
tentatively, on a bed of straw.

It isn't any one individual per se; it's the layers
of human thought that append themselves to an idea
and set its entire life course.

Back two thousand years,
blue sky met the ochre sand
in a perfect line.
It was the wandering shepherd who triggered all the fuss —
the celebratory gesturing of his hands

Space

Space is not neutral.
It depends on who inhabits it
and how.
Here, it's imbued with impulse.
It breathes.
It is wooded with dark creatures —
though it might just be me.
It's a dimension I'd rather not think about.
I enter anyway. Being human.
A residue of violence clings to the windowsill.
You and your wife, why did you?
And repeatedly, according to the news.
The space is not neutral.
Nor is the one embracing the crib.
The room vomited.
It bled, peed, shat.
It made gurgling baby sounds.
It screamed its lungs out.
Day and night.
The space shifted to Intensive Care.
I enter because. In a way I have to.
Now it's a tangle of circuitry.
It breathes mechanically.
In, out, in, out.
It is unresponsive to light.
Painting it would be out of the question.
Utterly.
Even thinking it.
But being human.
I'd imagine a landscape.
One long, yellowy line.
With my pencil,
          vigorously,
I'd strike it through.

Light

...be happy!
and with your beads on, because it rains.
— Frank O'Hara

What good are they sleeping
in their darkish bedrooms?
I want to tell them before it's too late:

Morning, like a coral bloom,
floats on the waves.

Take out your fingerpaints,
stewards of the drifting fronds
and radiant sun along the rippled floor —

see that fishing boat at the end of the wharf?
The muck of river stones in your hand

is a good thing.

Context

The child, straddling her mom, bends
to the rapids,
her fingers like buds awakened
to the shaggy wind,

the metallic sprint of river water.
The ducks shoot past

and she cups her hand, wanting in.
But the mother's restraining arm
tells another story, rooted in her fears
of the disturbed ecosystem, the quagmire of
what's below or beyond

or overhead, threatening.
Even the dense clouds buttressing the sky
are unravelling, strand by strand.

Collage

The first-drawn breaths,
filling the air with movement.

A green apple touches four walls
like the body at the womb
of a tree, opening itself.

Pale yarrow waves,
sprints down the street
from side to side, swaying
in the white light of eight o'clock.

I am more frightened of flowers than anything.

~

Every evening in the metropole
something brushes against your foot,
guides you so far.
But the heart wanders where it will.

Once, I saw you on the street and watched you
disappear,
so young, and already a genius.

The room is empty.
We are held by a moment
the colour of water.

Let me start over.

Time grew large, and then compacted.

~

The sound of a distant siren.
Above us, night repeats itself.
Pushed by an invisible hand.
This is the entranceway.
The clock runs in either direction.

The theatre's gone, the laundromat.
Your anger has fallen through a mirror.
I look at my palm.
It is quiet; you are warm.

~

Maybe when I'm 90, bent beyond recognition,
eyes unable to focus, I'll tell you something.

What happened was prophecy. Repeating
a slow sad dance, up and then down.

I think of you constantly at the door, that letter
in your hand. Cold as January rain.

Such was the conceit.

The hard blue feral spark,
the sky,

a sigh erupting where stars used to be.
Stand still and you can feel time collapse.

~

What you need to say has many rooms:

A man who smells of rotting mushrooms.
A man who may or may not own a truck.

That slide of eye, that wary glance.

August everywhere, but only
in this one meadow.

Saying *home*.
It has the weight of a stone falling.

II

An idea is only as good as its execution.
— *Kit White,* 101 Things to Learn in Art School

The Holocaust Tower

You lost your glasses at the Jewish Museum.
Autumn trees were unseasonably bright,
the plazas a patchwork of knackwurst
and graffiti, beer and bicycles and surreal
collectibles of days gone by:
gas masks, canisters, helmets and armbands,
the rare and the not-so-rare.
Items from the Cold War
in their original boxes.
Everything else was uber-real.
Real coffee to go.
Real people from everywhere,
waving their art around.

Three days we watched poetry films
from Norway, Canada, Egypt,
pixelated worlds composed and decomposed
in fifteen minutes or less,
the time it took the froth to settle on our coffee.
It's what happened afterward.
We were looking deeply into the eyes
of the oven-bound —
great, gaunt sockets. It was there, I think.
Neither of us noticed. Somehow your glasses fell
unannounced into the quiet sweep of tourists.

Or we were too focused
on the darkness at the end of the hall,
the absolute void of a stilled pavilion,
which lured me but swallowed you whole,
your silhouette disappearing
into the matrix of '44,
where your mother shivered inside a cattle car,
World War II exploding overhead.

Later, we found you a new pair.

School

The child slides down the long neck of the week into Friday.
Slouched at his desk he has a target on his forehead. The teacher
wants an answer. He shrugs it off, the way he shrugs off his
backpack. All this energy, trapped inside him, biding its time,
waiting for him to shed his chrysalis. Quietly he floats in the canoe
of thought, moved by its gentle ebb and flow. Downwind, familiar
sounds: the plash of a cast-off net, a fish hook trembling over
spangled water. It is mid-morning there, but over here the teacher
keeps at him, as though his brain were a cabbage she is helping
to grow. Smiling but firm, she says encouraging things like
"Shoot for the moon — even if you miss, you'll land among the
stars." He wishes she would see that he is not a dwarf planet.
If she cared an iota, she'd know about the swirl and eddy of
life around him, starting with his grandfather's cabin and the
long blue arms of the sky. He knows from memory the music
of frisky mosquitoes and snapping twigs.

Everything he needs is in the physics of the moving water,
translucent with fish.

The Hottest Car I Ever Drove Was a 1978 Monza With a V8 Engine and a Fuchsia Interior

But my nose, today, is in a novel
about an adulterous queen in her canopy bed.
Two-thirds in, I'm at the juicy bit,
where finally, after the light grazes
her shapely thigh,
after a life of slavish devotion to things,
she runs a simple comb through her lover's locks.

The lover is no porcelain doll.
She is a woman.
She burns
with every kind of unsettling weather.

The queen, however? Ambivalent.

"A single wind sends a boat adrift. And yet
it returns," she says. "The world is awry.
Desire, lust — neither of these
can set anything straight."

In fact, she understands little
except that time's always existed, and once
every few moons,
the sky balloons, vermilion.

I sort of know where this is going.

Like a leaf, she'll disintegrate into a thing
too small to name. Then she'll be shameless
about slipping off her silk bodice and surrendering.
She'll make a lover of night.

This, it seems to me, is a glimpse into God.

5 a.m. the Day of Your Mother's Funeral

for T.K.

If the day can't stand at half-mast,
it should remain, at the very least,
in partial shadow.
Only the barest inkling
of sun on the horizon.
Dwindling poplars should lament
the night's bitter aftertaste.

I'm headed east
in the florid darkness of a motor coach
shaped like a bullet, long and silver,
with passing flashes
through the windows —

showy billboards advertising carry-on luggage
for "that trip of a lifetime,"
cars with their receding tail lights
floating down the highway.

The world should stay this way the entire day,
dusky, sleepy, nothing its true colour;
the sky washed out
or sealed in an atmospheric coma.

When I blink again, clouds become the haunches
of an Arctic wolf advancing on its prey.
And what I take for the scattering light —

it's the charged particle of a wilful star
severing ties with the Earth.

Night Drive

As a child, I wondered about the muted lamplight
of the homes we passed as winter blazed.
The trick was not to fall asleep but to notice everything
in its brevity,
to catch the fleeting details of this or that:
a widow in a black dress, folded in on herself;
the wire hook on a naked wall
where someone's photograph has been taken down;
           little hatching signs of spring:
a gutter's teary icicle,
Mother inhaling deeply, singing
"She'll be comin' 'round the mountain when she comes…"

Once while we were driving, darkness splintered
into a million shards. Apparently we had struck a moose.
For weeks afterwards, I couldn't go near the basement.
The groaning furnace terrified me.

It is not a parenthetical world out there.
There is no simple way, for anyone, to go on.

Barkwoodby

— *After the painting* Above Lake Superior *by Lawren Harris*

Nunced clouds in five shades of hawtone.
An acqualous sky.
Skinny birches, brittier than most,
amburned by sun.

And voilà, the first surprise of spring:
shadows following the early snow,
gnarly roots of a snaking momonon.

The rest, you anticipate:
                    cherry blossoms,
giddened chuts of light,
scrots and dreaks of runnah.
All whispering
their emplet of solitude.

You've read Thoreau.
You recognize these pabled woods,
the moratern bludge
at the heart of every mountain
echoing its name.

Note

Tempera on Yellow Post-it
76 x 76 mm
(c. 2007)

You asked what I wanted this year
and I wrote "a cure,"
meaning any of the gruelling roads ahead.
Give me colicky seasons
and barbarian wind,
a writhing snake pit of stars.

What I want?

The weedy landscape
to collapse under the total sum of our being.

I want earthquakes and flash floods,
the unstoppable melt
of the dwindling glaciers.

I want you to take my hand and walk me
into the hurricane.

Introduction to Reiki

I wasn't, as they say, in the centre
of my life. But neither was anyone else
in the room,
chakras as clogged as our kitchen sinks.
We sat on the floor in stocking feet,
the Great Lotus filling our lungs.

One spoke of a churning
in her solar plexus,
another complained of a constant buzzing.
            On her wedding night,
she'd waltzed with her mate
under the fiery stars as cosmic debris
slid off them like rain.
But, eventually…

How people repeat the same mistakes,
was what we were thinking.
How a wife becomes a woman trapped
inside a radioactive cloud.
The Master twirled his wand of incense,
lifting our spirits.
My arches rooted to the ground.

It could have been a different weekend.
I could have been home in my slippers,
watching the Middle East implode.
Maybe I'd have broken down —
or swept out my garage.
Or caught the airwaves issuing a ceasefire
as the Earth's plates screeched to a halt.

This isn't so much about growth as a door
swinging open on the almost-dead.

Watching You Do T'ai Chi at Dawn

There's a burgeoning gap in the sky
as the clouds part above you,
in a distant realm
where sand lice and the latrine stench
of declining civilizations are virtually non-existent.
And like me, you're here,
but somehow you're not.

What I admire is not you
or the hulking freighter of what you know;
what's awesome is your coexistence
with the flea-sized minutiae of the galaxy,
you, graceful as a gull,
the perfectly stilled world
in your gaze.

It could be any day, but it's Friday.
Tomorrow we return to the city.
And so I study you
as an artist scans the planes and curves
of a partially lit stone.
But there's no great revelation.

The earth doesn't shake or rumble
with meaning as a rosy light settles
over the beach.

       There's just one crested wave.
And then another, and another.

THE ELEVENTH HOUR
(2020)

Instead there were little daily miracles, illuminations,
matches struck unexpectedly in the dark.
— *Virginia Woolf,* To the Lighthouse

Augury, I

The world is calling out for the world.
In the throat, an endless mountain,
words rising, the shapes unnatural,
a bluish bit of hush at the centre.
See the circling hawk: there is longing here.

And So, the Wind

I awoke to handfuls of light,
the cool wind pressing through a window.
Undulating curtains.
My blood sugar spiked, energy pumped
through my body's meridians.
I was as open
as new life blinking into the sun
for the first time,
a blank slate, ignorant
of our long, dark, collective history:
sooty traces of the Industrial Revolution
coating our lungs. Unaware
of the naysayers and conspiracy theorists,
fascists and colonizers
fighting like wolves for the scraggy earth,
however fucked up;
I marked an X on the great,
white, marble museums
rigged with dynamite and set for extinction,
erudite civilizations
detonating into the atmosphere.

And so, the wind.

It came to me, in a shallow breath, that nothing mattered,
nothing at all,

it addressed me by name, this flush wind,
it rippled through me,
it rose and fell like a tribe of women, dancing.

This Finite Moment

After a dozen years
our hibiscus is saying goodbye.
Last week,
we moved it outdoors for some natural light.
The sickly thing mustered the last of its will
and produced a stunning blossom.

The doctor says my anxiety will fade
when I learn to accept that life is finite,
when I firmly banish the idea of tomorrow.
Consider that astounding bloom, he says —

flamenco dancer in the final performance
of her career. Disregard her sweaty bow
as the curtain falls,
the dressing room where she sits at the mirror
removing her makeup.
Her rush to catch the last bus.
Ignore the Scotch she pours
as she tallies up her personal regrets.

Remember, instead, her Spanish dress
igniting the stage, her racing heart,
her *duende*
orbiting the nucleus of time.

Autobiography

I sometimes imagine my distant relations
running away from the Ottoman Turks,
crossing the ocean on a lower deck
with battered suitcases,
leaving the familiar
cedars and olive groves to sow a life
in the burgeoning needle trade.

I found their travel documents,
sepia portraits of moustached men
in Sunday suits, hair smoothed back,
courage in their eyes.
New as dawn
they docked in America, jostled and steered
through a crowded facility to pass inspection.

The rest is patchy.

Young, on their mettle they board a train
for Montreal,
work their immigrant fingers raw,
peddling dishrags, haggling for a cent
so that years hence
I might find myself

lolling in the hammock of a warm afternoon,
rent paid up, industrious pen
weaving history from scraps.

Augury, II

Years ago — how quickly time can pass us —
the quiet theatre of our lives.
Dunes, green shadow, rumpled blanket:
everything beginning that moment.
Which is longer, winter or the distance
between them? It dawns on me that perhaps
you are not coming.

City Fountain, Remembrance Day

Water shoots to a potent height,
the V of "victory" heralding other words —
"stealth" and "triumph" — that also begin
with the decorated letters of the alphabet.

Today
slim pickings for the pigeons perched
on the marble soldier:
broken helicopters shed from trees,
shrunken wreaths
on the cenotaph built for the men of Passchendaele.

A female figure flanks the base,
gazes ahead —
armoured Athena with the firm resolve
of my cherished *Sitti*,
who, at thirteen,
not yet menstruating,
drove the Turks from her father's land,
earning her place in family lore.
To hear it, she mounted a stallion
bareback,
and defeated the entire Ottoman Empire.

I don't spring from an ordinary well.
Age has settled in my joints and hips,
slowed my pace,
which my girlish heart did not expect
in the make-out car with Crazy Mike who'd never die,
no matter what.
It's almost been a year, my Love,
a hundred more for those who fell in the Great War.

Timeline

He announces, by George, he'll draw again —
Genghis Khan, Napoleon, Lawrence of Arabia.
Men who split the earth on horseback,
who banished the enemy,
who galloped through the desert,
fending off death.
Warriors,
not husbands with heartburn
schlepping groceries from the car.

In his youth our father sketched: portraits of Mom
before the cancer infiltrated.
A good sport, he managed the fort
until new and improved she returned from the hospice —
illness downgraded to a green alert,
a blip on the radar, a problem solved.

Dad's problem: giving his all, the skin off his back —
and arms and legs and torso,
the skin from his ears and the nape of his neck,
and why not take a few fingers while we're at it?

He never had time to draw,
transporting us to the movies and back,
correcting homework,
taking instruction, moving the house
a smidge to the left, a smidge to the right.
He was too busy making art out of life,
saving our bacon,
saving his nickels for the church coffer,
some for the starving kids in Africa.
He skimped on electricity
so we could all graduate college, as planned.

Kvetching over cost, he registers for class.
Refusing help,
extricates himself from the passenger's seat
and away he goes with his wooden cane
up the steps of the retirement home,
plastic bag with his sketchbook and a sandwich
bumping his knees.
88 now, he has all the time in the world.

The Black Box, Unpacked

When I think of an aircraft losing control,
the worst images come to mind:
the collective, uncontained horror of faces,
luggage exploding in the cargo hold.

Even in the glass-half-full scenario,
which I have read about — stillness
in the fraught seconds before impact —
it is a haunting underwater ballet.

Like an odourless gas undetected,
an aquarium glow floods the cabin
while the unsuspecting drift to sleep.
Strangers, they are conjoined, row upon row
floating through space.
They don't dream of tomorrow or next year
or the year after that.
They do not dream, end of story —
freed from time, the seasons and their cycles,
the moon, the tides.

Seems that when a plane goes down at that speed
people experience total blackout —
            the Earth's affairs redacted entirely.

The irony of the Exit sign isn't lost on me.

Status Update

You know this fundamentally
      without a book or calculator,
      or school professor —
a meaningful day is surviving,
hauling your kill
back to shore, siphoning the fat,
tossing the rich organs into a pail,
thanks issued
in the wide berth of sun across your face.
A higher power might factor into the equation,
but most of it is you
waking up
on the vast curvature of the earth's surface,
gauging the wind,
wrestling the dense algorithms of snow.

Speaking of Death

If I had my druthers
I'd pick December under a sheepskin throw.
In full view, attending to me,
a constellation of earthly possessions:
eyeglasses, ginger tea,
The Complete Poems of Emily Dickinson.
Logs flaming in the stone hearth.
Hung from a nail, a winter scene
framed in mahogany —
horses trotting through fresh snow
or a Christmas cabin nestled in the woods,
smoke drifting sideways from the chimney.
Riches for the eyes,
and for the ears, as well:
the Great Mass in C minor, swelling,
rising as it would from a dour cathedral.

On the other hand,
I could slip away in summer sheets,
white Egyptian cotton, of preference.
Nibbling on toast
I would lie in bed, pale as a moth,
gaze longingly through the soft sheers
as sunlight fades over an English landscape —
woolly hilltops brushed with lavender,
chittering birds perched like quarter notes
on a thatched roof
before taking flight along the path of the stars.

Arthur

Whenever I sit to write
the same old sparrow lands
on the outer ledge of my window,
beyond the desk
where my keyboard lies,
waiting for inspiration.
It is Arthur, always Arthur
with his distinct markings,
the matchstick hues
of the drained soil in late November.
He's like a nervous man in a tweed coat,
scurrying across the street
with a newspaper under his arm,
and he may not be a sparrow at all
but he is definitely Arthur.
I would never mistake him for another.
He arrives gently on the wing of dawn
and awakens me to my higher self,
the little flame that, upon death,
never extinguishes
but vanishes momentarily in a sudden
wind, to appear once more
in the strangest of places
when nature returns in the arms
of a cloud. I believe
that long after my ashes have cooled,
that dear bird will find me again
wherever I am, in the web of silence,
the way he finds me now,
with my sleeves rolled up
and some tea in a pot, steeping.

Augury, V

I forget things, as I have forgotten time
and the heart, which beats hard
after the long hall of mirrors, less impressive
at the seams, gathered, pinched as though
each thing on earth were
breath by breath, thought by thought
an incremental withdrawal.

ACKNOWLEDGMENTS

First, to the editors of the individual collections, in chronological order: Michael Harris, George Amabile, Sue Sinclair, Endre Farkas; and to Arleen Paré for this selected volume and her comprehensive and insightful foreword.

Thank you to the publishers of the individual collections: Nuage/Signature Editions, Brick Books, and Ekstasis Editions.

To the magazines and anthologies where some of these poems, or versions of them, first appeared: *The Antigonish Review*, *Prism International*, *The Malahat Review*, *Matrix*, *geez*, *An Anthology of Canadian Poets for Turkish Resistance*, *Vallum*. Thanks to Alison Moss who produced some of the poems from *Snow Formations* for the CBC-Radio series "Home and Away" on *Between the Covers* (2001).

Gratitude to friends and colleagues who have provided guidance and support over the years: Mark Abley, Robert Allen, John Asfour, Raymond Beauchemin, Antonio D'Alfonso, Gaston Bellemare, Alain Cuerrier, Michel Gagnon, Gary Geddes, Steven Heighton, Kitty McKay Lewis, Jeffrey Mackie, Elise Moser, Elaine Kalman Naves, Ken Norris, Denise Roig, Paul Vermeersch, Margaret Webb. And to Karen Haughian who saw something in my work and published my first book.

Thank you to Joel Silverstein, for humour, precision (and not getting us killed by a moose). But mostly, for friendship.

To my family for their love, laughter, and constant presence in my life. To Endre for being my rock and kindred spirit; to Alex for always daring me.

Finally, to the Conseil des arts et lettres du Québec and the Canada Council for their financial support of some of these collections.

Carolyn Marie Souaid, Montreal
September 2022

ABOUT THE AUTHOR

Carolyn Marie Souaid was born in Montreal in 1959 to first-generation Lebanese Canadians. Her ancestors immigrated to Toronto and Montreal in the early twentieth century and earned a living in the garment industry. Souaid spent the first five years of her life in Ste-Hyacinthe on the Yamaska River, sixty kilometres east of Montreal, where she obtained a strong base in the French language. In 1966, the family moved to St-Lambert, an upper-middle-class suburb of Montreal where Pierre Laporte was kidnapped in 1970, thus precipitating the Quebec Crisis and the inspiration for Souaid's second collection, *October*.

During this difficult time, her parents always discouraged Souaid and her two siblings from associating with neighbourhood children whose parents were anti-French. They believed in Pierre Trudeau's bilingualism and all three children learned to speak both of Canada's official languages.

Growing up, Souaid attended English Protestant schools, but was embarrassed by her ethnicity: Diversity was not properly part of most communities in those times. She hid her mother's pita, hummus, and rolled grape leaves in her lunchbox because other kids thought they were strange foods. This discomfort stayed with Souaid into adulthood, and she had no interest in connecting with her Lebanese roots until 1992 when she began making arrangements to adopt her son, Alex, from Beirut. Since then, they have not been back for a visit; Lebanon has often been too volatile.

Souaid received her B.A. in English Literature from McGill University in 1981. Subsequently, she began a degree in Law, but dropped out early. After three years teaching in the North, she took her M.A. at Concordia University and chose poetry for her creative writing thesis. Although in high school Souaid hated poetry, she gravitated toward it when she discovered Charles Bukowski in her mid-twenties: "The way he gave a voice to the common man, the working class, the poor, the down and out, appealed to me. I enjoyed his offensive, in-your-face depictions of urban life in all its depravity. I wanted to write with his rawness. It seemed more real to me than the dry poems of the dead white men we had studied in school."

Her teaching career began in small Inuit communities along the Hudson-Ungava coast of Nunavik (northern Quebec), including Akulivik, where she taught with Michel Gagnon, her future husband, a staunch Québécois nationalist from a small pulp and paper town near Sherbrooke. His blue-collar family was very different from Souaid's. They had only been married four years when Souaid began her Creative Writing degree at Concordia. Following her thesis, *Swimming into the Light*, she wrote *October*, her love letter to Canada. The first part deals with the story of the October Crisis from the perspective of a ten-year-old Souaid; the second part attempts to find a common ground with Gagnon. She says her goal in writing it was to find a solution to the French/English problem in Quebec, and in Canada. She and her husband divorced in 2008.

For over a decade now, she and her life partner, Endre Farkas, are each other's closest writerly companions. At the same time, they leave space for each other to manage their own artistic careers. During the pandemic, Souaid took online art courses and began to paint abstract landscapes, which, to her, have the feel of poetry. She thinks it's likely that in future, each art, visual and literary, will feed the other, making her a truly renaissance, multi-talented, creative artist in so many senses of the word.

— Arleen Paré